WHEN
Oceans
RISE

Scriptural Truths To Anchor The Soul

DANIEL HAMLIN

WESTBOW°
PRESS
A DIVISION OF THOMAS NELSON
& ZONDERVAN

Scripture taken from the NEW AMERICAN STANDARD BIBLE®,
Copyright © 1960,1962,1963,1968,1971,1972,1973,1975,1977,1
995 by The Lockman Foundation. Used by permission.

WestBow Press books may be ordered through booksellers or by contacting:

WestBow Press
A Division of Thomas Nelson & Zondervan
1663 Liberty Drive
Bloomington, IN 47403
www.westbowpress.com
1 (866) 928-1240

ISBN: 978-1-4908-7929-1 (sc)
ISBN: 978-1-4908-7931-4 (hc)
ISBN: 978-1-4908-7930-7 (e)

Library of Congress Control Number: 2015907080

Print information available on the last page.

WestBow Press rev. date: 05/08/2015

There are certain people in my life that I love to be around because they have spent a lot of time with God. Dan Hamlin is one of those friends. *When Oceans Rise* reminds me of the many meaningful conversations we have shared together. It is one thing to know about God, but there is a level of wisdom and insight that comes only from those like Dan who have experienced a long relationship with Jesus Christ. This book will bring you closer to the maker of the waves.

Bryan Jennings
Founder of Walking On Water Ministries

What a fun and encouraging read! *When Oceans Rise* is a sweet offering of life's most profound moments and lessons, as told by a young man learning to follow Jesus with reckless abandon and a surfboard! Set against the backdrop of an all-loving God and His promises, this journal-styled book is sure to encourage and inspire all of us who are trying to understand how to best ride the tides of life. There is real encouragement in these pages. Enjoy …

Brad Corrigan
Member of the band Dispatch, founder of Love, Light &
Melody

Dan has been a friend for years through his passion for Christ, surfing, and combining the two. *When Oceans Rise* is a personal journey of Dan's life integrating his faith in the real world, even his surfing world. Honest, challenging, heartwarming, with a sound biblical basis and insights that God has inspired him to, Dan challenges the reader to a more authentic walk with God. Thanks, Dan, for taking us all along the journey with you.

Brett Davis
International director, Christian Surfers

What a journey! As a surfer who follows Jesus, I found myself smiling as I read *When Oceans Rise* because I could relate to a lot of these stories. There are times we end up in the impact zone in life, but the best part about being in the impact zone with Jesus is that He always delivers you out of it with much more faith and blessings. That's the fun and why we continue to paddle back out.

CJ Hobgood, 2001 World Champion of Surfing, World Surf League competitor

To my Lord, God, and Savior Jesus Christ. Anything good about me or any good thing that I've done in life is simply a result of Your presence in my life. May You always receive all credit, glory, praise, and honor. You have not only saved me, but Your friendship has also changed my life. I wait in utmost anticipation of seeing You face-to-face one day. I love You.

CONTENTS

Foreword...xi

Preface.. xiii

Acknowledgments..xv

Introduction...xix

Chapter 1   Though the Fig Tree Wither 1

Chapter 2   Where the Rubber Meets the Road..................... 13

Chapter 3   The Divine Decree 25

Chapter 4   The Essential of Abiding...................................... 37

Chapter 5   Let the Dialogue Begin.. 49

Chapter 6   Identity Crisis 61

Chapter 7   The Heart of the Matter 75

Author Biography.. 85

FOREWORD

When Oceans Rise was a joy to read. Being a longtime friend and pastor of Dan Hamlin, I could hear his voice, sense his humor, sincerity, and humility in every chapter. As a born influencer of young people, Dan has an amazing devotional life that translates into his everyday walk as a believer. Being the son of a senior pastor, he has an intrinsic appreciation for the Scriptures and the Holy Spirit. Jesus said, "The words that I speak to you are spirit, and they are life" (John 6:63). The stories contained in the following pages are communicated by a heart that has learned that we serve a personal God who takes the chapter and verse of Scripture and turns it into life.

An easy book to read, *When Oceans Rise* will encourage you to seek intimacy with God, increasing your awareness of His abiding presence and love, with a reminder of obedience as you learn to hear His voice.

Pastor Patrick Sparrow
Shouts of Grace Church
Arroyo Grande, California

PREFACE

This book has been the result, more or less, of a number of mistakes I've made in life. If you are like me, often the lessons learned through error are the ones that seem to have a lasting impact. I'm not really sure why it is, but I've noticed that some of my greatest insights into God's Word have been revealed by the Holy Spirit through mistakes I've made. It's not always the case, and I'm definitely not advocating a life of purposeful mistake making in the name of gaining scriptural knowledge; that is not a good idea. Rather, my hope is that sharing some of my mistakes and the lessons I've subsequently learned through them will help keep others from falling into the same traps I've stumbled into.

This book, however, is not simply about my mistakes. Another desire for me in writing this book is to stir in us an appreciation for God's Word and how one of the Holy Spirit's roles in a Christian's life is to open our understanding to Scripture. The most profound truths I've ever found in Scripture have not come from years of reading commentaries and historical reference books; they have come by simply spending time in God's Word and allowing the Holy Spirit to be the teacher. One reason the Spirit is given to us is to guide us into all truth.

Throughout my life, the Bible has proved to be my most valuable possession. It has provided comfort in times of distress, hope in times of despair, wisdom in times of confusion, and perhaps most importantly, understanding toward the heart of God. When oceans rise, the Bible is an unfailing anchor. I have come to the conclusion that God's Word is the single most important physical resource known to man. God's Word remains forever. Every truth found in the Bible is an eternal truth, so the importance of reading the Bible cannot be overstated.

I've been fortunate enough to be able to do some traveling in my life. I've spent a lot of time in foreign cultures amid foreign customs. One thing I can say without doubt is that God's Word transcends all barriers and borders. It speaks every language and is not only an eternal truth but a universal truth. It applies to every single living being in existence. When we begin to grasp how big and how powerful God's truth is, we begin to see the importance of understanding what He has spoken to us. As we understand His Word, we get a sense of the magnitude of His love toward us and realize that His love is the answer to all of life's problems.

Hopefully some of the truths I've learned and share here will ring true with someone who reads this.

ACKNOWLEDGMENTS

This book likely would not have happened without encouragement and support from a number of friends and family members. Somehow the words *thank you* seem to fall short of expressing the depth of my gratitude, but nevertheless I wanted to take this opportunity to thank those who have helped me along the way while writing this book.

My parents, Craig and Jennifer Hamlin, and my brother, Matthew, have provided unwavering support, encouragement, and love that I will forever be grateful for.

Mom, throughout my life you have never wavered in encouraging me to write, and you've spent countless hours editing my work. This book is as much a result of your hard work as it is a result of mine.

Dad, your walk with the Lord is a continual source of inspiration. You have been one of the greatest resources in my own walk with the Lord, and I'm eternally grateful for your example.

Matthew, I've looked up to you since we were kids. I'll never forget all the times you looked out for me and how you would even translate for me when no one could understand what I was saying because of my speech impediment. I'll always be grateful for you.

Grandma (Marjorie) Hamlin, I can't thank you enough for all the support, help, and love you have given me throughout my life. Please know I'm grateful.

Winfield Bevins, you encouraged me to take the step of faith to write this book, and then you spent countless hours along the way selflessly helping me. Thank you for your support.

Jesse and Whitney Hines, I recognize that I am truly blessed to have the kind of friendship you have given me. Thank you for the selfless kindness and support you have shown me.

Paul and Allie Smith, you have been a continual source of support and inspiration. Paul, thank you for all the time you spent mentoring me when I was growing up and for showing me the importance of having fun in life, even when times get tough.

The Sparrow families—Pat and Terri, Mike and Jan, Josh and Makela, John and Lenae, Zach and Alie (Hinrichs)—you have all provided support and encouragement when I've needed it most. You have made me feel like I'm part of your family, and I'm eternally grateful.

Robbie Domingues, thank you for your friendship, support, and faithful heart to reach people with the love of Jesus. You encourage me daily.

Bryan Jennings, my time at Walking On Water has proved to be an instrumental season in my life. Thank you for your friendship and trust.

The Lokkart family, thank you for your kindness and generosity and for letting me use the cabin. It was a very inspirational place for me.

The Raubingers—Kyle, Nathan, and Jordan—thank you for your steadfastness and encouragement. You inspire me daily with your desire for Jesus.

To all the photographers who contributed, thank you for your trust and your expertise.

The terrible thing about an acknowledgment section is that there is not enough room to thank everyone I'd like to, so I've tried to simply name those who had a direct impact on the completion of this book. So to all my family I've left unnamed (but never unappreciated), I am forever grateful for you and the bond we share. And to my family of friends, particularly those on the Outer Banks and those on the Central Coast, please know that words cannot describe how blessed I am by your presence in my life, and I will always thank God for you.

INTRODUCTION

When I was about five years old, I remember telling my mom that I wanted to write a book. I didn't even know how to read or write at the time, so I'm not sure what made me think I could write a book. But my lack of literacy didn't really occur to me. I got my mom's old typewriter out, loaded a page, and began to type all the words I had memorized at that point in my life. Roughly six words later, my masterpiece was finished, and completely incoherent.

In my early twenties, I heard the Lord tell me to start writing, so I started a journal. At first I would write down every little thing that happened to me each day, but I soon found myself losing interest in writing about things such as what I ate for dinner. Shortly after this new initiative to write, the Lord taught me that what I feel is a very valuable lesson—a lesson I am still learning today. In Joshua 4 the Lord told Israel to set up stones for remembrance after He had parted the Jordan River and led Israel safely across it. The stones were in essence markers of His faithfulness. If future generations began to doubt Him or to question His faithfulness, they could go back to that place where

God had proven Himself before and have a visual reminder of His faithfulness. I realized my writing had become, more or less, stones of remembrance for me. Whenever He orchestrates circumstances, answers prayer, provides healing, or teaches me something of His eternal truth, I now do my best to record it as a reminder of His faithfulness.

It is amazing the faith that is garnered when we recall all the times that God has proven active in our lives. A few years ago, shortly after my uncle had passed away, I began to question God's faithfulness. I went to the only source on God that I knew would not deceive me—the Bible. One thing I learned during that time in my life is that even when we are faithless, God remains faithful. The Lord began to speak to me through Scripture, and as He did, I began to have peace again in life. He also reminded me of all the times He comforted me during past trials and how He has always been with me. My journals contained my very own testimony of this fact.

Over time as I went back through my old journal entries, I noticed that so many of the lessons the Lord has taught me are interwoven with each other, almost like stanzas in a poem. I've done my best to relate here a number of the truths the Lord has taught me throughout the course of my life and the circumstances that led to those revelations—from being trapped in a cave as it filled up with water while surfing to the Holy Spirit opening my understanding to Scripture.

Throughout my life I've noticed that our walk with Christ is just that: a walk. We don't reach some plateau where we know all mysteries and understand all enigmas. It is a continual walk, a progression of relationship. We can't make God into a formula; we must get to know Him personally, and as we do, we begin to recognize His interaction in our lives. Something He has taught me along this walk is that He is always speaking; I just need to listen for His voice. When we are told in Scripture that His Word is living and active, it is a literal statement. His Word is always speaking. The revelations He continues to reveal through Scripture are evidence of this. As you read through these pages, my prayer is that the truths He has revealed in His Word will similarly impact your life as they have impacted mine.

PHOTO BY MATT LUSK

Chapter 1

THOUGH THE FIG TREE WITHER

A SEASON OF LOSS

On April 29, 2012, I was sitting in my parents' family room debating whether I should go to the beach to surf or not when I got a phone call that would change my life. It was a sunny, warm, Sunday afternoon—not really the type of day I would have imagined my life to change so drastically.

The phone call was from the hospital emergency-room doctor. My uncle Jim Hamlin, an avid cyclist, had been out on his usual Sunday bike ride when an out-of-control motorist hit him from behind. The doctor didn't give any details over the phone; he just said we needed to get to the hospital as soon as possible.

My mom and I raced to the ER. The ten-minute drive felt like an hour. I tried telling my mom not to assume the worst, that Jim would be fine. We prayed, and I remember thinking that surely God wouldn't let him die, that surely something this terrible couldn't be God's will for Jim or for us.

When we got to the hospital, the doctor explained to us that Jim was brain dead on impact. He was still alive on life support, but he likely wouldn't remain alive much longer. He told us to say our good-byes.

I walked into Jim's room to find him lying on a bed covered with a blanket and with a breathing tube coming out of his mouth. I grabbed his hand and started talking to him. I told him how much he meant to me and how much I loved him. Jim was a big part of my childhood; I can scarcely remember a camping trip that he wasn't a part of. To see him lying there, on the verge of leaving this world, was surreal. I tried not to cry within Jim's view. I somehow thought that if he saw me crying, he'd know how severe his condition was and stop hanging on. The nurse told me he couldn't hear or see me, but I felt otherwise. Between fits of sobbing and disillusionment, my family members and I told Jim how much he meant to us.

Jim had been hit at 1:00 p.m., and at roughly 7:00 p.m., he went home to be with Jesus. He was only fifty-eight years old and in excellent physical health.

Jim's death was the third passing of someone I dearly cared for within six weeks. One friend, only twenty-one years old, had passed from a massive asthma attack, and the other friend, also only twenty-one, had passed from a yearlong battle with a rare form of cancer. I had barely experienced death in my life, and now, within a matter of weeks, I was surrounded by it—so much so that I felt almost numb to its bitter taste.

But as time went on, I started processing the sudden losses in my life. I began wondering why death comes to some people seemingly too soon and what these events had to say about God and His love and character. These events renewed in me a thirst for Jesus and made me long for the childlike confidence in His character that I had while growing up but that now seemed to be wavering.

In writing this book, I'm not trying to seem as though I've reached a higher plane in my spiritual walk or that I know a step-by-step process to answer life's most challenging questions. I'm simply trying to share what I believe Christ has taught me about who He is and His character. I've found in my life that when oceans rise, when doubts seem to overwhelm and circumstances seem hopeless, the Word of God is a steadfast companion and a solid foundation that won't be moved.

ETERNAL INTENTIONS

There are times in our lives when the Lord seems to have forsaken us. My uncle's death was one of those times. I had no idea the pain, anxiety, and barrenness that death could bring.

When I was a child, the Lord graciously revealed Himself to me in a very real way, so I grew up knowing and believing that God was with me in every breath I took. I felt Him present in every season of life. Obviously, there were times when He seemed nearer than at other times, but regardless of my circumstances, I had a general sense that He was always there. But suddenly, although doctrinally I knew the correct answers to the questions and doubts arising in my mind, I felt that perhaps those answers weren't good enough.

My friends and family, who were experiencing the same loss, were asking the same perplexing questions, and I felt that any explanations I gave as to why such tragedies happen were utterly insufficient. And to be completely honest, I still don't feel I've grasped the fullness of this mystery. But thanks to God's Word, I feel as though I've come to terms with it.

> When I pondered to understand this, it was troublesome in my sight until I came into the sanctuary of God. (Psalm 73:16–17a)

The only way to understand life's most perplexing problems is to spend time in Jesus' presence. No other resource known to man can equip an individual the way time with Jesus can. It is an inexhaustible resource that will fill even the deepest recess in a person's aching soul and provide a comfort that yet remains to be fully and accurately described with words.

Psalm 73 is a perfect example of this. Asaph, the author, was in absolute confusion as he looked around and saw the wicked prospering. They prospered so much that Asaph even questioned whether living a life following after God was worth it. It seemed that no matter how hard he tried to do the right thing, it simply didn't matter. Those around him who chose wickedness seemed to be prospering while he seemed to be constantly experiencing God's chastening. Who among us hasn't felt this way at some point in life? Who hasn't looked around in frustration at how evil and destruction seem to prosper?

For weeks, I pondered the meaning of the deaths of my loved ones. Each of them had a relationship with Jesus. Each of them was deeply loved by their friends and family. Each of them seemed to have died too soon. Why?

Psalm 73 appeared to hold the key to understanding such questions. It's only when we enter the presence of God that we begin to have a clear view of life and its mysteries. There is no formula to life; it is about relationships, and God intended for us to live relationally with Him. Until we spend time with Jesus, we will never experience the peace that God promises.

With the insight from Psalm 73, I began seeking answers in God's Word. A person begins to know and understand his or her mate only after they have spent countless hours together in conversation and intimacy. You begin to understand a person's character and who he or she truly is in his or her heart of hearts by spending meaningful time with that person. In the same way, we will only get to know Christ if we spend time with Him. We will only hear His voice if we take time to learn His voice. This is not a new concept, but if we are sincerely seeking answers and truth in our lives, this is the only way we can be sure of finding them.

> Though the fig tree should not blossom, and there be no fruit on the vines; though the yield of the olive may fail, and the fields produce no food; though the flock may be cut off from the fold, and there be no cattle in the stalls—yet I will exult in the LORD, I will rejoice in the God

of my salvation. The LORD God is my strength, and He has made my feet like hinds' feet, and makes me walk on my high places. (Habakkuk 3:17–19)

Habakkuk is a bit of an obscure prophet in the Old Testament, but we will gain much by reading and taking to heart what he had to say. Habakkuk was given a vision of Israel's impending judgment and the distress that had already begun for his people. He was also assured of God's deliverance for and kindness toward the righteous—those who lived relationally with God. Habakkuk knew as certainly as the sun would rise each day that the distress the Lord had predicted would come upon Habakkuk's land. The people of Israel, like all of us, would certainly reap what they had sowed.

It would be easy to understand if Habakkuk decided to give up. I'm sure he thought, like Asaph the psalmist, that he'd wasted his time in keeping himself pure in a land of wickedness. But God revealed something about His character in Habakkuk's vision that we ought to always remember. He showed us that even in the midst of impending doom, He is able to bless those who walk with Him. He is able to keep them and comfort them in dire circumstances.

When life was full of distress for Habakkuk, when oceans began to rise, he recognized the character of God and remembered that God is true to who He has always been. Though his land would become barren, Habakkuk still praised the Lord because He was still worthy of it; Habakkuk knew, despite his circumstances, that God was bringing about an eternal good and would not forsake him.

All of life's distresses have come as a result of man's sin, or man choosing to live life apart from God. So whatever catastrophe happens in life, no matter how heartbreaking it may be, it was not God's original intention. His original intention is evident in the account of the garden of Eden. He intended to live with us in a personal, face-to-face relationship in which we would not experience heartache. But none of us can change the past, so we are destined to live in a world that is full of sorrow and confusion.

None of that, however, changes God's character or intentions. He still eagerly desires to bless us and continually does so. Habakkuk recognized these facts and chose to praise God for who He is, not for what his life's circumstances were. In Habakkuk 3:19 he acknowledged that in the midst of darkness, God is able to make us rise above it and walk in security.

In the midst of barrenness, God brought His eternal perspective to Habakkuk. He will not forsake His children, and Habakkuk knew that even when times seem especially hard, the Lord would provide for, strengthen, and comfort those who call on His name. With this perspective, Habakkuk could confidently say in spite of the circumstances surrounding him, "I will rejoice in the LORD, I will joy in the God of my salvation."

Like Habakkuk, we too can have this confidence in God. We can rejoice in the midst of dire circumstances. God has not changed, and neither has His love for us.

A PERSONAL HOPE

In Jesus' earthly ministry, He taught an important principle that is easy to forget. In the parable of building a house on a firm foundation, it is easy to grasp that Jesus is saying we must build our lives upon Him. He is the Rock, the firm foundation that will not be shaken. But in this same parable, Jesus also tells us that regardless of which foundation you build upon, you will face storms in life. Each house experienced the same distress, but only the one built on the rock stood. The storms that hit the houses were not minor rain showers; they were floods, torrents, and slamming winds. In this life, those who follow Jesus will experience the same kind of physical heartache and distress that those who don't follow Him will. This isn't meant to discourage anyone; I'm just trying to point out that God never said life would be trial free. In fact, He says the opposite. But He does promise us, "He will never leave us nor forsake us." In this is great comfort.

> For I know whom I have believed and I am convinced that He is able to guard what I have entrusted to Him until that day. (2 Timothy 1:12b)

In 2 Timothy Paul disclosed to us his secret to living confidently in the midst of life's storms. He was not confident in himself, and neither was he confident in his works. His confidence lay in Jesus. But why was he so confident in Jesus?

If you look at his life, on the surface it would seem as though Paul had every right to question Jesus. In his second letter to the church at Corinth he described trials he'd faced in life that would make most of us squirm at the thought of enduring. He was imprisoned multiple times and beaten so many times he'd lost count. He was stoned and left for dead and shipwrecked three times (one of which resulted in spending a night and a day floating at sea). He'd suffered hunger and exposure as well as many other major trials, and yet in spite of all these things, he claimed his confidence was in Jesus. Was Paul insane? Many of his contemporaries claimed he was. But Paul was as lucid as you and I; he simply had a relationship with Jesus that kept things in perspective. We often lose our perspective because we don't spend time with the one capable of helping us see life as it truly is. Jesus is the true lens of life.

Notice what Paul said to Timothy: "For I *know* whom I have believed and I am *convinced* that He is able to guard what I have entrusted to Him." That is a telling statement. Paul *knew* Jesus. He'd spent time with Him. He'd talked with Him and told Him his own frustrations and hurts and daily made Him a companion. Paul spent so much time with Jesus that he had an intimate knowledge of Jesus' character. All those trials that Paul experienced grew Paul's faith. In every horrific circumstance that Paul faced, he was learning that Jesus was someone he could count on.

Though most of Paul's trials were a result of his service to Christ, he never blamed God for experiencing them. Paul recognized that there are two opposing, yet not equal, forces in this world—God and the Devil. Whenever someone commits to advancing the kingdom of God on earth, the Devil will do his best to frustrate that person's commitment. We must not blame God for the acts of the Devil; this is a common tactic of the Enemy. The Bible tells us that greater is He who is in us than he who is in the world. Paul knew it wasn't God who was harming him, but as a result of experiencing such trials, he also came to know that it was God who was *with* him in the midst of them. He had experienced Jesus' presence and comfort in the heart of his most troubling times in life.

Paul's second letter to Timothy was one of his last earthly writings. In it we find the root of his steadfastness. As I said, he didn't just believe in Jesus; he *knew* Him. It was this close relationship with Jesus that sustained him in one of the loneliest times of his life.

Paul went on to say in this letter to Timothy that when he was put on trial for the sake of the gospel, not one person stood by his side but all deserted him. It's sad to think that after all Paul had done, all the people he served and ministered to, not one of them stood by him in support. But it did not affect Paul in the least. He said, "But the Lord stood with me and strengthened me" (1 Timothy 4:17). Paul's steadfast faith was a result of his intimate relationship with Christ. All his needs were met in the person of the Holy Spirit, whether companionship, support, strength, or whatever else he faced in life. He looked only to Jesus. And we can have the same type of relationship with Christ as Paul did. Jesus is eager to reveal Himself to those who desire to know Him.

APPLICATION QUESTIONS

1) Do our circumstances or trials change who God is?
2) What was the apostle Paul's secret to steadfastness in the midst of trials?

PHOTO BY COLIN NEARMAN

CHAPTER 2

WHERE THE RUBBER MEETS THE ROAD

Though trials can be some of the most miserable times of our lives, they can also be used to bring us into a deeper relationship with Jesus that can be reached in no other way. In life's trials we are forced to come to terms with the faith we profess. Do we believe in who God says He is when all of our circumstances seem to deny His goodness? Do we believe that the end of the matter will be better than the beginning because God promised us it would be? Do we believe Jesus came to heal us and to save us regardless of our past mistakes? Do we believe that when oceans rise, God will not let us drown? Unfortunately these are questions that can only be answered when we have gone through trials.

When I was twenty, I attended a Christian Surfers International conference in Santa Cruz, California. During one of the conference's afternoon breaks, I decided to go surfing. Santa Cruz generally has better waves than my home stretch of coast around Pismo Beach, but this day was stormy and the waves were not very good. Still I had made up my mind to paddle out. As I began to put my wetsuit on, I heard the Holy Spirit tell me to spend time with Him instead of going surfing. I wrestled with this for a second, knowing it would mean I wouldn't get a chance to surf that day. I decided I'd surf first, and then if I had time afterward, I'd spend it with the Lord. I had no idea what would result from my disobedience and selfishness.

After what could only be described as a miserable surf session, I decided to call it quits and head back to my car. I had caught a couple of bad waves, gotten frustrated by the incessant current that kept me paddling the whole time, and ended up cold and discouraged. As a result of the current, I exited the water a good distance from where I had parked my car, which meant I would be walking back to the parking lot along the edge of the rocky coastline. I sheepishly made my way back, the water lapping over my feet as I walked. Then it happened.

There are moments in life that stay with you forever; this would end up being one of those moments. In the blink of an eye, the ocean literally began to rise all around me. The next thing I remember, I was sitting in the back of a cave with my head throbbing as the cave filled up with water. A tidal surge had caught me with my head down as I walked along the edge of the cliff-lined shore. By the time I realized what was happening, it was too late. A wall of water had thrust me to the back of a cave that formed in the cliff's side.

The only thing I thought to do before the impending impact was call out to God for help. And that's exactly what I did. "God, help me!" I exclaimed. The next thing I knew, I was looking out through a twelve-inch gap of air between the cave's ceiling and the water's surface. The tidal surge was pinning me to the back of the cave.

As panic started to grip me, what seemed like a million thoughts raced through my mind, but one in particular stood out. I had ignored that gentle urging of the Holy Spirit not to surf and foolishly paddled out anyway. Before I had time to even assess my surroundings, I felt myself being rushed toward the opening of the cave as the tidal surge retreated. Acting purely on instinct, I swam as fast as I could with the current, and just as fast as I had been swept into the cave, I was swept out of the cave.

Hands down, it was one of the most humiliating experiences of my life as a surfer and one of the most embarrassing experiences of my life as a Christian. I had made a downright stupid mistake, and the only one I had to blame it on was myself. I knew the cave was there but paid no attention to my surroundings. And even worse, I had chosen to disobey the Lord and as a result had gotten myself into a life-threatening situation.

BEAUTY FOR ASHES

A man was there who had been ill for thirty-eight years. When Jesus saw him lying there, and knew that he had already been a long time in that condition, He said to him, "Do you wish to get well?" The sick man answered Him, "Sir I have no man to put me into the pool." (John 5:5–7)

The experience in the cave has always stayed with me. It's obviously one that won't soon be forgotten, but shortly after the incident took place, I felt as though the Lord intended to teach me something through it (other than the obvious one about obeying!). I searched the Scriptures, seeking some sort of verse or story that would bring a revelation as to the meaning of it all. The years began to go by, although I found great comfort in a number of Scriptures regarding the Lord's faithfulness in delivering us from trouble, I still felt as though there was a deeper lesson I was to learn from the incident. Then one evening as I sat in a Bible study listening to the passage in John 5 being read about the healing at the Pool Bethesda in Jerusalem, the Holy Spirit began to open my understanding and reveal a great truth about who He is. I finally felt as though the incident in the cave made sense.

In chapter 5 John describes a pool in Jerusalem called Bethesda. Near this pool, we are told that a great multitude of sick people lay in wait for an angel of the Lord to come and stir the pool's water. Whenever the angel did this, the first person who entered the pool would be healed of whatever disease he or she had. We are told that at this pool there was a man who had been ill for thirty-eight years, and for thirty-eight years he had no one to help him reach the pool in time to be healed.

Though I had read this portion of Scripture many times before, on this particular occasion certain details began to stick out in my mind. For instance, this poor man had been ill for thirty-eight years, and not one person in all of Jerusalem felt enough compassion for him to help him. I wondered at this! Why would nobody help? Surely if this man had been asking for help for thirty-eight years, eventually someone would have assisted him. But no one did. Why?

John continues in his account (of what happened at the Pool) by telling us of the exchange this man had with Jesus after He had made him well. Jesus found the man in the temple and said to him, "Behold, you have become well; do not sin anymore, so that nothing worse happens to you" (John 5:14). At this verse I felt the Holy Spirit open my understanding as to why no one would help the sick man. Because Jesus instructed the man not to sin anymore so that nothing worse happened to him, we know whatever illness this man had suffered from all those years was a result of his own actions. He had done something thirty-eight years prior that put him in the state he was in. The reason no one helped him began to make sense to me.

It was often thought in the culture of Jesus' day that an illness was a result of someone's sin. In John 9:2 Jesus' disciples asked Him regarding a blind man, "Rabbi, who sinned, this man or his parents, that he would be born blind?" If the man's sin had indeed caused his tragic condition, then you can begin

17

to understand the societal and religious mind-set that would deny him of any help or compassion. You see, whatever sin this man had committed that resulted in his illness, it was so offensive that no one in Jerusalem felt as though he deserved help. It must have been widely known what he did, and the general feeling must have been that he got what he deserved. They would help someone who deserved help but not this man.

But Jesus came to show that the Father has always been about the business of redemption.

No One Is Beyond Redemption

I believe Jesus chose this man out of all those seeking healing at the Pool Bethesda for a specific reason. I believe He chose this man because He knew the people, particularly the religious leaders, felt as though he was beyond redeeming. He wanted to show everyone that it doesn't matter what sins we've committed in our past; He came to grant us salvation and give us a new future.

Jesus in essence took the one person society had labeled as unworthy and the least deserving of compassion and showed mercy to him. It was a bold statement to those watching as much as it was a proof of His authority. And it speaks volumes of the Father's character. It reveals His true heart toward us and shows us that no matter what we've done in our past, He is still actively seeking to come into our lives if we will let Him. Jesus asked the sick man if he wanted to be made well; He gave the man the choice as to whether or not he wanted Jesus to intervene.

Many of us feel as though we have to get our lives in order before we can come to Jesus—that we have to clean ourselves up. But Jesus demonstrated His unmerited and incomprehensible love for us in His dealings with this man. He also showed us that even if we are in a self-inflicted state of utter despair, there is hope in Him. He has come to lift us out of the pit of our own folly. Even if those who have watched us grow up and run headlong into ruin condemn us and tell us we are beyond redemption, Jesus desires to show us compassion.

As I pondered this section of Scripture I remembered my incident in the cave. It was a result of my own actions and my own disobedience. I had no one to blame but myself for ending up in the back of that cave, and there was no one who could have helped me. Just like the sick man at the Pool Bethesda, I had brought my circumstances upon myself. Yet God saved me that day. He didn't shake His finger at me, saying, "I told you so, Dan; you're just getting what you deserve." He showed me that He was there to help even though it was my own fault. He allowed the water to retreat and brought me safely out of the cave I'd been washed into as a result of my disobedience.

No matter what situation we've gotten ourselves into, Jesus is ready and willing to save us. He eagerly desires to give us a new future and heal the brokenness of our past. It's part of who He is, a deep part of His character. Although our peers might disdain us, stating that we do not deserve to be helped, Jesus picks us out of the crowd to redeem us.

19

Daniel Hamlin

HOPE BEYOND HOPE

The account in John 5 of the healing at the pool also reminds me of the life of Job. But unlike the man at the Pool Bethesda, Job's circumstances were not a result of his own doing. He did not do anything to bring on the calamity that befell him. But just like the man at Bethesda, Job had no one to help him. In the midst of the worst time of his life, when God had seemingly abandoned him, Job stated, "Though He slay me, I will hope in Him" (Job 13:15). This is perhaps the most profound profession of faith that a mortal man has ever uttered. Job knew that despite his circumstances and despite the fact that people told him God had forsaken him, God could not deny Himself. Job trusted in who God *is*. Job knew God's character, and he knew God would remain true to His character.

King Solomon, the wisest person to ever walk the earth besides Jesus, wrote,

"The end of a matter is better than its beginning" (Ecclesiastes 7:8a). The man who was healed at Bethesda found a life of redemption and a personal relationship with Jesus when all was said and done. Job's life was more blessed after all the calamity had passed than it was before it began, and more importantly, he gained a deeply intimate relationship with God that he could not have experienced had he not gone through the trial.

If we will trust Jesus, we can be assured that no matter what we are going through, the Lord is working it all together for good and has something better planned for our lives than our immediate trials. Whether they are tragic like Job's, self-inflicted like the man at Bethesda, or even the result of stupid disobedience like my incident in the cave, we can rest assured that if we turn to Jesus, the end of the matter will be better than the beginning.

There is no better example of Ecclesiastes 7:8 and Job 13:15 going hand in hand than in the life and death of Jesus. As the disciples sat bewildered at the death of their Lord, God was working out something that would be the single most important event to humankind. Imagine the utter despair the disciples must have felt as they watched Jesus, the One in whom they had placed all their hope and trust, being crucified. But the horror of Christ's death would soon be replaced by the eternal joy of His resurrection. Had the disciples known this, they would have realized that the hope that is found in Jesus transcends even death.

Job understood this, though he may not have understood all of God's dealings with him. He knew that not even death could conquer the hope that is found in Jesus. Even when things are at their bleakest, and it would seem God is nowhere to be found, for those who hope in Him, God will make the end of the matter far better than its beginning.

In his daily devotional book *My Utmost for His Highest*, Oswald Chambers notes the existence of "clouds" or trials in a believer's life. He says, "Clouds are those sorrows or sufferings or providences, within or without our personal lives, which seem to dispute the rule of God. It is by those very clouds that the Spirit of God is teaching us how to walk by faith."[1]

We often find, like Job or the man at the pool, that in life's most difficult times our view of the Lord becomes clearer. Jesus' distance to us hasn't changed. He is ever with us, but trials have a way of sharpening our focus on Him if we let them. The resurrection of Christ couldn't have happened without the death of Christ. It was on the cross of Christ that God's heart of love was displayed open and unobstructed for us. If we let God have right of way in our lives, He will bring about something miraculous and amazing through our lives' trials. May we take comfort in this and never lose our hope in Him.

---

[1] Oswald Chambers, *My Utmost For His Highest* (Urichsville, Ohio: Barbour Publishing, Inc., 1963), July 29.

APPLICATION QUESTIONS:

1) Do our past mistakes affect God's love for us?
2) What are some good things that come out of trials?

PHOTO BY CHRIS BURKARD

CHAPTER 3

THE DIVINE DECREE

Over the years I've been employed in an eclectic assortment of occupations. For two years in my late twenties, I worked as an instructional assistant in a special education classroom for kindergarten through third-grade students. It was one of the most emotionally draining jobs I've ever had, but it was one of the most rewarding and fulfilling jobs as well. I often recall the kids I instructed with great fondness and cherish the memories I have of that time in my life. I'm sure I learned more from them than they did from me.

Shortly after I had started that job, I had a particularly enlightening car ride to work one day. On the drive I had the realization that I had a great responsibility on my shoulders in working with these kids. I was in a position to forever alter these kids' lives for the better or for the worse. When you're as young as these kids were, the impact of a single word of encouragement or discouragement is immense. The weight of the responsibility began to overwhelm me. Suddenly my mind was flooded with anxious thoughts and "what-if" scenarios. What if I wasn't as patient as I should be, or what if I wasn't as encouraging as one of the kids needed?

As I drove, I went through all the scenarios of how I might fall short when thankfully the Holy Spirit interrupted my thoughts. He reminded me of Proverbs 10:12: "Hatred stirs up strife, but love covers all transgressions." He began to speak to my heart with this verse. I knew that as a human I was destined to fall short. At some point in my position working with these kids, I would make a mistake; it was simply a fact of life. But with this verse, the Lord assured me that if I kept my heart right, then all would be well.

God's love for us was what brought us a Savior in Jesus. His love provided a way for us to be redeemed, effectively covering all our transgressions when we accept Christ. As Christians we are called to show Christ's love to the world; we are His ambassadors, and we are supposed to represent what He represents. Jesus was the embodiment of love, and He calls us to demonstrate His love to the world. I took the instructional assistant job because I felt the Lord wanted me to share Christ's love with the children I would be working with. It wasn't to help kids learn to read or teach them how to throw a ball; it was to share with them Christ's love as best I could. As long as I kept that as my objective and focus, then any mistakes I made along the way would be covered by the love of Jesus.

No teacher, parent, or mentor in life will be able to do a perfect job. But those who demonstrate a Christlike love for others can take comfort in the fact that Jesus' redeeming love will cover our transgressions. The power of Christ's sinless blood is what takes that which is un-right and makes it right. It's His sinless blood that is able to provide sufficient payment for our transgressions. When we allow His love to have right of way in our lives, we can be assured He will work all things together for our good, even our mistakes.

BLESSED ASSURANCE

I felt overwhelming relief as I drove to work that day when I began to realize the implications of this—not only in regard to the kids I was working with but also in regard to all relationships in my life. I did not have to worry about past failures or potential future ones; I could let both rest in the knowledge of the power of Christ's love. It's amazing to think that the love Jesus showed the man at the Pool Bethesda—the love that healed him and covered his past transgressions—is the same love that He offers us. His love is the same today as it was before the world began, and just like He demonstrates throughout Scripture, He desires to cover our mistakes in His redeeming love, heal our brokenness, and give us rest from our anxieties. It is part of who He is, just one aspect of His eternal love. So let's look at love and the reality of what it means to love someone.

LOVE IS NOT A FEELING

The term *love* is often thrown around these days in reference to God, regardless of what religion one may profess. The word has been so misrepresented and overused that it seems to have lost much of its meaning. Love ought to be a sacred thing, but today it is used to sell movie tickets and write pop songs. But this shouldn't surprise us. The Bible tells us in 1 John 4:8, "God is love." To have a true understanding of love is to have a true understanding of Jesus, and by that understanding we then know who God is. If the Devil wants us to be confused as to whom God is, he simply needs to distort our view of love.

First John 4 goes on to say, "By this the love of God was manifested in us, that God has sent His only begotten Son into the world so that we might live through Him. In this is love, not that we loved God, but that He loved us and sent His Son to be the propitiation for our sins. Beloved, if God so loved us, we also ought to love one another."

This Scripture explains why we can trust the love of Christ to cover our mistakes. No love that this world professes has the power to pay the price for our sins except Christ's love. In other words, no love has enough value to make compensation for our transgressions in life other than the love of Jesus. His sinless blood is the only thing with enough worth to cover sin. Jesus willingly offered Himself and His sinless blood in exchange for our salvation, and He did so because of love.

To say that God forgives us because He is love is not entirely accurate. His love is what compelled Jesus to sacrifice Himself for us, but forgiveness is granted on the basis that Christ's blood is a sufficient ransom for our sins. When we ask Jesus into our lives and accept the forgiveness provided through His blood, then God's Spirit indwells us and the love of God begins to fill us. Through us the same love that empowered Jesus to endure the cross is at work in our lives and is manifested to the world. This is why the Devil is so adamant about perverting our view of love. If we do not understand love, then we cannot properly share God and His salvation with a perishing world. It is also why it is so important to have a proper understanding of love. To gain a proper understanding of love, we must look to Jesus and the life He lived.

LOVE INCARNATE

When you look at Jesus' life, study what He taught, contemplate who He associated with, and think about the acts He accomplished, one can only logically conclude that He is the manifestation of love. No other figure in all of history displayed the type of love for mankind that Christ Jesus did. Love may be mocked, ridiculed, laughed at, or even denied, but it cannot be ignored. Love of this great magnitude demands a response. When we personally encounter this love, we all must make a choice: for or against. How we live our lives is directly related to our response to this love. One of the Devil's lies is that voicing our encounter with Jesus (love incarnate) might be offensive to some and so we should not do it. The offense does not come from love but rather from the denial of it. Let them be offended, but don't let love be silent in our lives.

To hear it said that all religions have the same love as their basis and therefore all faiths are equal is to have no real understanding of what love is or rather who love is. There is only one Jesus, only one God, and thus only one love. If someone claims to have love but denies Jesus and His gospel, that person does not have a correct knowledge of love. Or if perhaps someone acknowledges Jesus but also gives equal credence to another religion or religious leader, then he or she misunderstands love and is subsequently misrepresenting it.

It is popular when speaking of relationships to say that love is a feeling. But this sadly is untrue. Love is not a feeling; love is a choice. God chose to make mankind. God chose to have fellowship with us. God chose to pursue that fellowship even when we separated ourselves from Him, and He chose to make Himself known to us when we were lost. He chose to pay whatever the cost would be to make it possible to regain fellowship with us. He chose to love us. And when we rebelled and denied Him, or sinned against Him time after time, still He chose to love us. He chooses to love us. If love were simply a feeling, then it would be easy to hurt others or to discredit one another. It would be a perfect excuse to end a relationship or to deny Jesus. This is why the Devil is so desperate to misrepresent love.

True love has to be a choice. It cannot be a mere human feeling or impulse. What I feel about someone today may change tomorrow if that person annoys me in some way. There is no way for a relationship of any kind to last if love is simply viewed as a feeling or emotion. We must continually choose to love, just as Christ demonstrated in His life a continual choosing to love us. I'm sure Jesus did not *feel* like loving His disciples as they all deserted Him in the hour of His despair.

At any moment throughout His earthly life, including His arrest and crucifixion, Jesus could have simply said, "That's it! I've had enough; I don't feel like doing this anymore." And humanity would have been eternally lost. But He didn't. He made a continual choice to love us, no matter the cost. A proper understanding of love is essential for our growth in Christ as well as for our battle against the Devil and his schemes.

LOVE ETERNAL

During my time working as an instructional assistant, there was a particular kid who was quite hard to be around. He dealt with a number of mental and psychological issues that no doubt contributed greatly to his, at times, horrendous behavior. It was not uncommon for this child to hit or swing at teachers when he was asked to do something. He often would go into fits of rage where he would turn desks over, pull pictures off the wall, spit, bite, hit, or kick anyone who tried to calm him down. He often spit on me, hit me, kicked me, and even bit me. On one occasion at lunch recess, a teacher saw him playing in a zone that was off limits for the kids. She simply asked him to move into the proper area, and he proceeded to walk up and hit her. The teacher was stunned but thankfully unharmed.

I had an extremely hard time being around this kid, let alone loving him. But through this child the Lord taught me a great deal about His love toward us. I've often treated the Lord like this student treated others, with contempt and anger for no good reason at all. There's been many times in my life when

I have claimed to know better than God and tried to force my own will in a particular situation. Like that troubled student, I rebelled at any sign of God's concern for me. But God showed me that His love is not like the world's love. It is not based on behavior or merit or emotion. It is an eternal love, a love that does not depend on our acceptance or rejection of it. He loves us because He has chosen to eternally love us. However, God's love for us—though eternal, unmerited, and not dependent upon us—does not turn a blind eye to our behavior or provide a consequence-free existence. In His love for us, He has given us the freedom to choose right or wrong, and we subsequently are responsible for our choices. My prayer for our lives is that we will choose to love the way God has chosen to love.

Another common misunderstanding of love is to think that because love is a choice, we must ignore a wrong committed when we choose to love. This is incorrect. We do not ignore the offense, but rather we forgive the offender. We do not ignore the wrong committed or try to justify the offender; we are to simply love the person in spite of the offense. This can be exceptionally hard. It is not easy to love someone who has wronged you. In fact, the only way to truly be able to love in this way is by God's Holy Spirit living in us and transforming us into the image of Christ. The more we allow the Holy Spirit to reign in our lives, the more we are transformed into who God intends us to be and the more power love will have in our lives as a result.

THINK DIFFERENTLY

When Jesus started His earthly ministry, one of the first lessons He taught us was how essential it is to have a proper understanding of God and His eternal love.

In Matthew 4:17 we read, "From that time Jesus began to preach and say, 'Repent, for the kingdom of heaven is at hand.'"

When Jesus says "repent" in this verse, most of the time it is thought He is simply saying, "Confess your sins and stop sinning." It's often translated "to turn 180 degrees." These are both correct teachings, but they only begin to give the full implication of what Jesus was saying. One of the translations of this term *repent*, means to "think differently." When He tells us to repent, He is saying in essence, "You must begin to *think differently.*" Jesus is saying that heaven is within our grasp, but we need to begin to think differently.

Heaven could accurately and basically be described as the place where God and His creation dwell together in perfect fellowship. We've already learned from 1 John that God is love, so it can be concluded that when we reach heaven, we will finally know and experience love in perfect wholeness. So when Jesus says that heaven is within our grasp, He is also saying that a true knowledge and understanding of love is not only possible, but it is also essential.

In order to gain this understanding, we must change the direction of our thinking. This world's standards and laws are different from heaven's, so we need to replace the way this world has taught us to think with the way Christ teaches us to think.

The world says take; Christ says give. The world says judgment; Christ says mercy. Paul calls us ambassadors of Jesus. Political ambassadors are not under the laws of the kingdoms in which they live; rather they remain under the laws of the kingdoms they represent. Since our citizenship is in heaven and we are ambassadors for Christ here on earth, let us abide by the laws of our heavenly homeland. Jesus tells us the first step is to stop thinking the way the world does and start thinking the way Christ does. As we do this, we will begin to have a proper understanding of love.

APPLICATION QUESTIONS

1) How is God's love different from the world's love?
2) Is love a feeling or a choice?

PHOTO BY CHRIS BURKARD

CHAPTER 4

THE ESSENTIAL OF ABIDING

I worked with the Walking On Water ministry for a number of years, and it was a blessed time in my life. In 2003 we produced an evangelistic surf video titled *The Outsiders,* and we were premiering it to thousands of people along the East Coast of the United States. The Lord was blessing the outreach and was moving large numbers of people to accept Him as Savior at each stop on the tour. We were overwhelmed at the grace and favor the Lord was showing us.

As you can imagine, the days were hectic, filled with hours of driving in a cramped RV, the almost daily task of setting up and tearing down the equipment for each premiere, lots of late-night dinners, and practically no personal space or alone time. Don't get me wrong—it was an amazing time, but also a very busy one. Though I'm by no means perfect in my devotional time, I try to spend at least a little time with the Lord before I start my day. When the tour started, I kept up with my daily devotional time fairly well, but as each day passed and I got more and more worn out, I slowly began to fill that time with other things—namely sleep. It was easy for me to rationalize this because we were in the midst of a very successful time of evangelism. I remember thinking that it wasn't that big of a deal that I wasn't spending my daily time with the Lord because I was doing ministry for Him, so He would understand.

No Substitute

> But supposed Him to be in the caravan, and went a day's journey; and they began looking for Him ... When they did not find Him, they returned to Jerusalem, looking for Him. (Luke 2:44–45)

Things continued this way for about a week. But then one afternoon as we drove north in our little RV toward our next stop, I found myself unable to sleep, so I decided to "catch up" on some of the reading I'd missed. Somewhere in Georgia I read the passage in Luke 2 that tells how Jesus' parents left Him in Jerusalem after they had made the pilgrimage there in order to observe the Feast of the Passover.

My first thought was how could somebody who was entrusted with raising God incarnate lose Him? That seemed ridiculous to me, almost laughable. But then I felt the Holy Spirit expound this Scripture to me, and I realized that their mistake is a common one we all might make. It was a mistake I was making at that very moment. You see, His parents had gone to do what they were supposed to; they faithfully served the Lord by observing the Passover. They sincerely sought to honor the Lord. But in doing so, they unknowingly made the mistake I was making—a mistake we all are at risk of making. They assumed Jesus was in their presence, instead of making it a point to make sure they were in His presence (v. 44). I assumed that because I was involved in a successful ministry campaign that my own personal time with the Lord wasn't a necessity. When we're doing service for the Lord, it's often easy to assume that Jesus is in our presence. We lose sight of the whole purpose of serving the Lord—to be in His presence. I was humbled by the Lord's reminder to me not to lose sight of why I was on the trip.

OBEDIENCE, NOT SACRIFICE

Scripture tells us that God desires obedience rather than sacrifice (1 Samuel 15:21–23). It doesn't matter to what extent we spend ourselves in service for the Lord, if we are not obedient to Him, our service profits us little. We can spend all of our strength and energy in ministry, we can surround ourselves with godly people and godly activities, and we can do all kinds of good but still miss the point of it all. In that RV as we drove north from Florida to the Carolinas, in spite of the success of the ministry I was in, I realized I was still missing the point.

Jesus has an interesting depiction of service in John 12. He says, "If anyone serves Me, he must follow Me; and where I am, there My servant will be also; if anyone serves Me, the Father will honor him" (John 12:26). Notice how Jesus says that if we want to serve Him, we must first follow Him. Joseph and Mary lost sight of Jesus in their striving to serve. I lost sight of Him during my service for Him. If we follow Jesus as He leads, we will never lose sight of Him because He will always be in front of us, not behind us. We must always keep Jesus directly in front of us where we will not be in danger of losing focus on Him.

Another fascinating detail about Jesus' description of service in John 12 is the fact that He says, "Where I am, there My servant will be also." Proximity determines successfulness in service. Our success depends on being in Jesus' presence. There are many great things being done in Christ's name today, but they lack power and substance because they were born out of a sense of sacrifice for the Lord rather than obedience to Him. Christ wants to spend time with us; He wants us in His presence. He is a personal God who desires a personal relationship with us. Scripture says that in His presence is fullness of joy (Psalm 16:10–11), so it is there we will not only be truly fulfilled, but as a natural result of being in Christ's presence, we will also be successful servants. Please don't misunderstand me; I'm not saying ministry is bad, but the Lord has always been more concerned with the state of our hearts rather than the works we accomplish.

The underlying theme of both of these Scriptures (Luke 2, John 12) is that of abiding. We must abide in Jesus' presence if we want to be spiritually fit. Abiding denotes a continual dwelling, an uninterrupted state of communion.

THE SECRET

We are told in Psalm 91:1, "He who dwells in the shelter of the Most High will *abide* in the shadow of the Almighty" (emphasis added). To dwell somewhere is to live there, to make our home there, to make it our abode. It is our comfort zone. The secret to successful ministry is not in campaigns or fundraisers; it's not in sacrifice or evangelism. It's dwelling in the Lord's presence, to abide in the shadow of the Almighty. As we do this we find that ministry becomes a natural side effect of time spent with the Lord.

Ministry should always be a result of our relationship with Jesus, not the other way around; our relationship with Jesus should never be the result of or be dependent upon our ministry. When Jesus called His disciples, He didn't simply hire them to spread His message. He invested in them personally and spent time with them individually. He built a relationship with each one that was so intimate He could joke and laugh and cry with them. He resided with them.

After Jesus had given the Great Commission to His disciples, as He was about to ascend into heaven, He stated to them, "And lo, I am with you always, even to the end of the age" (Matthew 28:20). Jesus did not expect the disciples to enter ministry without Him. He intended to always be with them wherever He led them. I take great comfort in the fact that He has not abandoned us. Even when my priorities get out of order and I lose sight of my Savior, or when I let circumstances overwhelm me and I forget to look for my Comforter, I know He is faithful to open my eyes so I can see clearly. He did it for His disciples on the road to Emmaus

(Luke 24), and He will do it for us today. To abide in Jesus means He is our comfort zone, not our surroundings or circumstances.

The Comfort Zone

I've found in my own life that the Lord has to constantly remove me from my own physical comfort zones in order to get my focus on Him and make Him my comfort zone. It's amazing how comforting the presence of a good friend can be.

When I was twenty, I went to Costa Rica on a short-term missions trip with Christian Surfers United States. During the ten-day trip we spoke at churches, did beach cleanup, held outreaches, and surfed some fun waves. About halfway through the trip, we had a particularly trying day. We were supposed to drive from the Caribbean coast to the Pacific Coast, a drive that we thought would only take us about half the day. The plan was to meet our contacts at a church in the town of Jaco, drop our stuff off, and then surf before dark.

After getting lost partway through the drive, we eventually made it to our destination of Jaco on the Pacific Coast. It was now late in the afternoon, and daylight was rapidly disappearing. We found the church we were supposed to stay at and realized that there had been some miscommunication in arranging our lodging for the evening. The church was not set up to accommodate our group, so now we had to find a hotel that would have room to house us and all of our gear. As the leaders of our group figured out what to do, the rest of us stood by, hoping things would get sorted out quickly.

Tensions were rising as everyone had an opinion on what we should do. I remember standing in the dirt road in front of the church trying not to get frustrated by the unforeseen circumstances when I heard a familiar voice call my name. I turned to see Paul Smith, one of my best friends from back home, standing there with a big smile on his face. He and a couple of friends were in Costa Rica on a surf trip and "just happened" to drive down the dirt road in front of the church at the same time I was standing there. We were only able to talk for about twenty minutes, but at that time in the trip, at that moment, those twenty minutes were exactly what I needed. The comfort of an old friend renewed my strength and resolve, and suddenly the inconvenience of our miscommunication in regard to lodging seemed quite minor. The Lord orchestrated that divine meeting with Paul and provided exactly the encouragement I needed at just the right time.

How astounding is it that we have the ultimate comforter in our Savior? No matter what circumstances we find ourselves in, we can find comfort in the presence of the Holy Spirit. In my situation in Costa Rica, the only reason my friend Paul was such a welcome sight was because I had history with him. I had spent countless hours of my life hanging out with him. We had a real friendship fashioned over time. And this is the same sort of relationship the Lord desires to have with us. The more time we spend with the Lord, the more intimate our relationship with Him becomes. The more we abide with the Lord, the more comfort we find in His presence and the more aware we become of His works.

PHOTO BY JOSH SPARROW

HIS PRESENCE IS ENOUGH

In the book of Daniel, we find four great examples of lives spent abiding in the Lord's presence. In the case of Daniel being thrown into the lions' den as well as in the case of Shadrach, Meshach, and Abed-nego getting cast into the fiery furnace, there is for us a great lesson to be learned from their responses to the perilous circumstances they faced. In both cases, none of them questioned God's fairness in their situations. They did not ask why such evil had befallen them. They did not panic or get hysterical at such unfairness in their lives. Instead they understood that the Lord was with them *in* their circumstances, and they took comfort in the knowledge of His presence. They knew He was with them even in the midst of tragedy and that alone was enough for them. They did not need answers as to why such events happened in their lives; His presence was all they needed.

I love how we are told that the Lord was with Daniel *inside* of the lion's den, and He shut the lions' mouths so that they could not hurt him while in the den with Daniel. God did not keep Daniel from being cast into the lions' den, but He went with him into the peril. The same is true for Shadrach, Meshach, and Abed-nego; He did not keep them from being thrown into the furnace, but He was with them *inside* the furnace. This knowledge that the Lord would be with them in their trials was all they needed. His presence alone provided all the comfort they needed to endure such hardships.

Shadrach, Meshach, and Abed-nego's response when told that they would be cast into the furnace shows the steadfastness of their abiding relationship with the Lord. They did not try to make a deal with God by asking for deliverance in exchange for obedience. They did not succumb to the temptation to put their own safety and wellbeing before God and truth. Knowing that the Lord was still with them in the midst of such misfortune was all they needed. They understood that God is very capable of performing miracles, but they did not make His miracles the reason for remaining loyal to Him. Their loyalty was based on personal relationship; they knew the Lord and felt the comfort of His presence. It did not matter what sort of threat they faced; no amount of peril could make them deny Him whom they knew personally. His presence was their comfort and security; the Lord's ever-abiding love was their hope.

The presence of the Lord is what should sustain us in ministry, in trials, and in triumphs. The presence of the Lord changes everything.

APPLICATION QUESTIONS

1) What is the purpose of service?
2) What is the secret or key ingredient to successful service?

PHOTO BY JOSH SPARROW

CHAPTER 5

LET THE DIALOGUE BEGIN

> God created man in His own image, in the
> image of God He created him; male and female
> He created them. God blessed them; and God
> said to them. (Genesis 1:27–28)

Notice in the account of the creation of man, the first thing God did was to bless man and converse with him. His first order of business with us upon our creation was not only to bless us but also to start a dialogue with us. This should immediately tell us two things. The first is that God desires to bless us; His intentions toward us are good ones. He wants what's best for us (Jeremiah 29:11). The second thing it tells us is that God has always intended for us to have a personal relationship with Him.

I believe there is a difference between a personal relationship with Jesus and a saving relationship with Jesus. I believe a person can have salvation by placing his or her faith in Jesus and what He accomplished on the cross yet still miss out on the personal aspect of the relationship. It is possible to believe everything the Bible says is true and to genuinely put our faith in Christ's sacrificial death and victorious resurrection but to never experience the joy of having one's own personal, intimate dialogue with God. We can mistakenly view God as unapproachable, or perhaps uninterested in our lives, and therefore never experience the very thing He created us for—to truly know Him and be known by Him.

I'm convinced the only true way to know someone is to spend time with that person, to interact with him or her, to engage and be engaged by him or her. I can read a man's autobiography and know everything that happened in the life of that person but still be a complete stranger to him. The only way to get to know Christ is to spend time with Him, to talk to Him, to learn His voice, and to get familiar with His personality. God is, and has always been, a personal God; He wants to talk with us. He gives us His Spirit so we will never be apart from Him. He earnestly desires a relationship with each one of us and will go to every extreme to give us the opportunity to experience that relationship with Him. From the moment He made us He has been speaking to us, pursuing us with a love so passionate that no human can accurately articulate it completely.

A RAVENOUS LOVE

Jesus says in John 4:23, "But an hour is coming, and now is, when the true worshipers will worship the Father in spirit and truth; for such people the Father *seeks* to be His worshipers" (emphasis added). The term that is used here for the word *seeks* can also be translated "hunts." The Lord literally hunts us; He pursues us in hopes that we will enter into the relationship He originally intended to have with us in the garden of Eden.

Before they sinned, Adam and Eve enjoyed daily life in God's presence. They talked with Him, they lived with Him, and they did life with Him. Ever since sin entered the world and created a barrier between God and us, He has been actively pursuing us in order to regain that intimacy with us. As a hunter stalks his prey, our Creator desperately seeks us in order to bless us. Second Chronicles 16:9 says, "For the eyes of the LORD move to and fro throughout the earth that He may strongly support those whose heart is completely His." It is a pursuit initiated by God as a result of His severe love for us.

The Lord will stop at nothing to bring us back into an intimate relationship with Him. And prayer is key in restoring our intimacy with our heavenly Father. It's hard to love someone you don't know, and it's hard to know someone if you don't talk with him or her.

My mom, Jennifer Hamlin, has been a tremendous inspiration in my life and in my walk with Jesus. I feel she captures God's ravenous love toward us quite profoundly in her poem called "The Hound of Heaven."

The Hound of Heaven
By Jennifer Hamlin

The Hound of heaven tracks my days,
Pursuing me through bleakest haze.
His wail of love sounds in my ears,
Freezing on my face the tears
That haunt my endless night.

With unrelenting pace He runs.
My desperate cry of pain He shuns.
I stumble on in bitter haste
While He would seem to love the chase
That fills my soul with fright.

Blinded by my stubborn fear,
I didn't see Him standing near.
Cursing at my weary fate,
I fall, too burdened by the hate
That set my soul to flight.

Noiselessly He kneels down.
With gentle hand He turns me 'round.
I marvel at His burnished face,
For streaming down are tears of grace
That cleanse my sullied sight.

And now my eyes can clearly see
The tenderness that called to me.
While carrying me upon His back,
He shields me from fierce attack
With great and glorious might.

THE COMFORT OF HIS PRESENCE

In the fall of 2000 I was attending Bible college in Southern California. It was an extremely intense time of growth in my relationship with the Lord. Up to that point in my life, I had never lived more than fifteen minutes from the coast, and I always had my family nearby for support. At Bible college I was living in the desert, an hour from the nearest beach, and about five hours away from my home and family. It was the first time I had lived on my own, and I was basically removed from all of my comfort zones.

To be honest, I had no idea how hard it was going to be for me; if I had there's a good chance I would have reconsidered attending the school. But as is often the case, when I look back on that experience, I can see the Lord's loving hand orchestrating everything for my benefit. There were a number of divine events that unfolded as a result of being there, and many of my most cherished friends and memories can be traced back to that time in my life.

There was one particular evening that will remain with me forever. It was during the middle of the semester on a particularly stormy and lonely night. The rain and wind only seemed to make the loneliness heavier. Though I had made some friends at school, none of them were very close. I spent lots of my free time alone and often just wanted someone to relate to. I experienced the tormenting and seemingly overpowering weight that is loneliness that so many experience in life. It is an intense and indescribable feeling, one I wish no one had to experience.

Add to this the fact that dorm life, noisy roommates, and cafeteria food don't provide the best environment for proper nutrition, so as a result I was in what seemed to be a constant cycle of getting physically sick and mentally discouraged.

Usually my outlet for stress and anxiety is surfing, but since my surfing time had been delegated mostly to the weekends, and sometimes not even then, I was finding myself getting deeply depressed and struggling with severe loneliness. There were times in that desert when all I wanted to do was look out at the ocean to watch it rising and falling, but I couldn't.

These struggles came to a head one evening. There was a little prayer chapel by my dorm that not many people used. I don't exactly remember what prompted me to go inside that night, but I found myself sitting alone in that dimly lit prayer chapel on a night that would change my outlook forever.

As I sat there, I listened to the sound of the rain and wind howling outside; then I began to pray. But it wasn't like my typical prayers; it was more personal than that. I actually began to just talk with the Lord, no pretense, no selfish motives, no religious jargon; just simple, heartfelt conversation with my Father in heaven. I expressed all I was feeling: my loneliness, anxiety, depression, frustration, and fear—I didn't hold anything back.

As I talked with the Lord, I began to experience an overwhelming feeling of peace and love. I felt the presence of the Holy Spirit there with me. The feeling was so intense that I started to weep, unlike any other time in my life before or since. I wasn't weeping from sadness or loneliness but rather from a sense of long-sought-after peace and comfort. I felt His intimacy; during that talk with the Lord, I poured everything I had out to Him and felt Him respond. I didn't hear a verbal answer—lightning didn't come down from the sky—but I knew

He had heard me. I knew the peace and comfort I was feeling were not only the Lord answering me but were also His Spirit there with me. He was with me in my loneliness, anxiety, and illness. I wasn't on my own; He was with me in everything. He had heard me and answered me, and He let me know that He understood.

I realized that no matter what our situation or circumstances are, the Lord is with us. He was with Adam and Eve in the garden of Eden, He was with those who called on Him throughout Scripture, and He was with me when I felt as though no one was. He had always been with me, eagerly waiting to comfort me; I just needed to sit down and talk with Him so He could.

I left that prayer chapel feeling as though a weight had been lifted off of my shoulders. Up to that point in my life, I had known Jesus was real. I had known Him personally and as Savior, but after that conversation in the prayer chapel, I knew Him altogether differently. I somehow knew from then on that He is always with us; the Holy Spirit is an ever-abiding presence waiting to be united with us, the closest of all companions. The Holy Spirit hunts us, and prayer is not merely important in our relationship with Him; it is vital. We cannot be intimate with God if we don't have an ongoing and personal dialogue with Him.

As I spoke of in a previous chapter, the apostle Paul was intimate with Jesus. He was so intimate with Jesus that he was able to take comfort in the fact that Christ was ever with him, even in a lonely jail cell where all his friends and companions had deserted him. He still felt the Lord's presence.

How was Paul so intimate with Jesus? What was his secret? He is very candid with us in a number of his letters as to where this intimacy came from. He writes to Timothy, "First of all, then, I urge that entreaties and prayers, petitions and thanksgivings, be made on behalf of all men" (1 Timothy 2:1). He writes to the Thessalonians, "Rejoice always; pray without ceasing; in everything give thanks" (1 Thessalonians 5:16–18a). Again he writes to the church in Ephesus, "With all prayer and petition pray at all times in the Spirit" (Ephesians 6:18), and to the Philippians he says, "Be anxious for nothing, but in everything by prayer and supplication with thanksgiving let your requests be made known to God" (Philippians 4:6).

Paul lived each day in communion with the Lord; he talked with Him often. Paul recognized that prayer is vital in a believer's life, and without it we are at great risk of being stagnant in our walk with Jesus and vulnerable to the Enemy's schemes. It's interesting to note too that a major theme in these prayer references I've listed is the attitude of thankfulness Paul expressed. A thankful and peaceful heart is a direct result of being intimate with Jesus. As we pray and meditate in the presence of the Holy Spirit, we are transformed inwardly. One of my favorite insights into the result of growing intimate with the Lord comes from Charles Spurgeon. He says the following:

> Nothing will so enlarge the intellect, nothing
> so magnify the whole soul of man, as a devout,
> earnest, continued investigation of the great
> subject of the Deity ... Would you lose your

sorrows? Would you drown your cares? Then go, plunge yourself into the Godhead's deepest sea; be lost in His immensity; and you shall come forth as from a couch of rest, refreshed and invigorated. I know nothing which can so comfort the soul; so calm the swelling billows of grief and sorrow; so speak peace to the winds of trial, as a devout musing upon the subject of the Godhead."[2]

THE GATEWAY TO INTIMACY

Spurgeon understood one of the great mysteries of our faith, which is the closer we draw unto God, the more life we experience. When we finally stop running from the Hound of heaven and allow ourselves to be captivated by Christ, we begin to experience life as it was intended to be: an ever-increasing intimacy with our infinitely good heavenly Father. But the only way we get to that place is by spending time with Jesus and growing intimate with Him. Prayer is our gateway to intimacy.

I find it interesting that during Jesus' earthly ministry, He explicitly taught and instructed the disciples on prayer. It's recorded for us that He gave the disciples specific instructions on this matter. We aren't told if He gave the disciples specific instructions on how to speak in tongues or on how to prophesy,

---

[2]   Charles Spurgeon, *The Immutability of God* (A Sermon delivered on January 7, 1855, at New Park Street Chapel, Southwark).

but we are deliberately given instructions to pray and then given an example of how to pray. Jesus doesn't tell the disciples, *"If* you pray;" He says, *"When* you pray." Prayer is not optional in the disciple's life. Remember in the account of Jesus overturning the money changers' tables in front of the temple, one of His outcries was that the temple was not being used for its intended purpose. He lamented in Matthew 21:13, "It is written, 'My house shall be called a house of prayer.'" If prayer is this important to Jesus, then it should hold the same importance in our lives.

APPLICATION QUESTIONS

1) How does prayer affect our intimacy with God?
2) Can we trust God's plan for our lives?

PHOTO BY CRAIG HAMLIN

CHAPTER 6

IDENTITY CRISIS

Identity is a big issue in most people's lives. We naturally want to identify ourselves and be identified with something. We often find our identity in our family, our significant other, our work, or perhaps our favorite hobby. We take an unspoken comfort in having a particular identity that is suitable to us. I remember as a kid I grew up playing baseball and basketball. As I got older, I began to identify myself as an athlete. In high school I played on the school teams for both of these sports, but when I was sixteen, I began to grow weary of high school sports and the politics that went along with them. My dad, who was a surfer, suggested I give surfing a try. So I did, and I loved it. But I remember it caused a great dilemma for me. I knew that if I were to quit high school sports and take up surfing that some of my peers would think I was changing—that I would no longer be one of them.

I'd quickly got hooked on surfing but tried to continue to play baseball and basketball to keep the status quo in my circle of friends. But as time passed, I became more immersed in surfing and more disenchanted with high school sports. I finally realized that surfing was what I enjoyed most and what I really wanted to do. I still liked the other sports, but I no longer wanted to participate in them. Looking back now, I realize how melodramatic it was, but I remember making a conscious decision that from that point on I was going to be a surfer and not a basketball player or a baseball player. I was going to be identified differently.

As the years have gone by and I look back on my life, I see how the Lord orchestrated that decision to take up surfing. It wasn't that He wanted me to identify myself as a surfer—quite the opposite—but He has used surfing as a tool in my life, and I can confidently say it was His will that I took up surfing. Surfing has been a gift in my life, but there have been times when I have worshiped the gift and not the Giver, identified myself with the gift and not with the One who gives the gift. I have allowed myself to lose sight of the reason the Lord gives us these gifts, or tools, which is to grow closer to Him and carry out His purposes. We find this evidenced in Moses' life.

WHAT IS YOUR STAFF?

> The LORD said to him, "What is that in your hand?" And he said, "A staff." Then He said, "Throw it on the ground." So he threw it on the ground, and it became a serpent; and Moses fled from it. But the LORD said to Moses, "Stretch out

your hand and grasp it by its tail"—so he stretched out his hand and caught it, and it became a staff in his hand—"that they may believe that the LORD, the God of their fathers, the God of Abraham, the God of Isaac, and the God of Jacob, has appeared to you." (Exodus 4:2–5)

I believe the staff represented to Moses what he identified himself as—what he was and what he did. He was a shepherd of flocks; that's what he knew, that's what he was comfortable as, that was his identity. But God asked him to lay it down, to surrender it. The Lord was asking Moses to give up the identity he had made for himself and become identified with God and with His purpose. It became a serpent so Moses could see what he was really holding onto.

As long as Moses held onto his identity without surrendering himself to God, the thing he clutched, the thing he identified himself by, the very thing that God intended to use in his life, would eventually turn into his foe. If Moses had worshipped the gift instead of the Giver, then the very gift intended as a blessing would become harmful to Moses. But Moses obeyed God and surrendered it, and when he did, God asked him to do an interesting thing: He asked Moses to pick it up again. Moses had to trust God in doing this. He had to have faith in order to grasp the serpent, and when he did it became a staff again. Moses' identity no longer was found in what he did or who he was; it was now firmly established in the One he had a relationship with.

The staff that, when left unsurrendered, had the potential to harm Moses was now an instrument by which God would perform many miracles within the hand of Moses. Moses now carried the staff not as a shepherd of flocks but as the shepherd of God's people. By surrendering himself in all aspects, he was able to have a relationship with God that few have ever experienced. The gift could be used as the Lord had intended for it to be used, and Moses was able to partner with God in bringing about His kingdom here on earth. What is the staff in our hands that God is asking us to lay down? I pray we have courage like Moses to surrender it and watch as God transforms it into an instrument used to advance His kingdom.

PHOTO BY COLIN NEARMAN

Daniel Hamlin

A CONSTANT SURRENDER

If you are like me, you might have to surrender something more than once before you really release control of it to the Lord. There have been many times in my life where I have tightly grasped certain gifts the Lord has given me, and when I do so, they lose their blessing. Notice in the account of Moses and the staff that God gave Moses a second sign. He instructed Moses to put his hand to his bosom, and when Moses did, his hand became leprous. I believe the symbolism here is great. I believe God was showing Moses that if he held anything in his heart greater than God, it would become a plague to him, even if it were the hand by which God was going to lead His people free from captivity. God is always more concerned with the state of the individual's heart than He is with the individual's ministry. He is a personal and relational God, with an infinite desire to know each one of us.

Multiple times the Lord has had to ask me to lay down surfing, to give it up for a time and release my hold of it. I really enjoy surfing, and if I'm not careful, it is really easy for me to make my identity in it instead of in the Lord. I have to take care that I'm not consumed by the gift but rather that my identity and focus remain Jesus.

At one time in my life, I felt the Lord ask me to give up surfing for a month. I had become conscious of the fact that surfing was beginning to consume me; I was identifying myself with the gift and not the Giver. So I set aside thirty days during which I would not surf. I'm not saying that something like this

66

is necessary for everyone to do, but at that point in my life I knew that I personally needed to relinquish my grasp on surfing and realign myself with God's plan. I wanted first and foremost to be identified with Christ, not a gift He had given me to enjoy. It wasn't an easy task for me. But after those thirty days ended, I felt a much greater freedom to enjoy surfing knowing that my identity wasn't in the gift or in the ministry tool but rather in Christ.

I had the privilege of working alongside Bryan Jennings during the early years of the Walking On Water ministry. Jennings is a former professional surfer who used his platform in surfing to start Walking On Water, a ministry that uses the sport of surfing to share Christ's love with people around the world. He went through a season in life that is a great example of laying down the gift in order to grow closer to the Giver, and when he did so, the gift was used as a tool to advance Christ's kingdom.

Bryan accepted Christ as Savior when he was a senior in high school at a Bible study he'd been invited to. The following weekend he won a professional contest that launched his surf career and gave him his dream of being a professional surfer. Two years later while attending Point Loma Nazarene University, he entered a prayer chapel to pray and heard the Lord tell him to give up surfing competitions for a year. He wrestled with this, knowing it would mean the end of his surfing career, but realized he needed to obey the Lord, so he gave up surfing contests for a year to focus on his relationship with Christ.

After the year was over, Bryan felt the Lord release him from his fast of professional surfing, and shortly after he received an offer from the surf brand G&S to surf professionally for them. Once again the Lord had given Bryan a career in surfing, but this time Bryan used surfing as a tool to share the gospel. He says of this time in his life, "The Lord wanted me to surrender the sport of surfing, especially professionally and competitively, to show me that He is more important than surfing. God has a plan for our lives."

THE MAGNITUDE OF OBEDIENCE

> For the report of your obedience has reached to all; therefore I am rejoicing over you; but I want you to be wise in what is good and innocent in what is evil. The God of peace will soon crush Satan under your feet. The grace of our Lord Jesus be with you. (Romans 16:19–20)

Have you ever considered the magnitude of our obedience to Christ? Paul tells us here that it reaches to all. In other words, our obedience has an effect on the whole world. Moses' obedience brought about deliverance for an entire nation. Because he obeyed the Lord's directive, the Lord was able to use Bryan Jennings to share the gospel with surfers worldwide.

What a remarkable concept to get a hold of. In 1 Samuel 15:22 we are told, "Behold, to obey is better than sacrifice." There is something in the heart of God that is moved when His children willingly choose to obey Him. Our obedience allows God unhindered movement in our lives, thus allowing for Him to move through us to carry out His purposes. It's His kingdom we want to advance, not our own, and our obedience partners us with Him in advancing it. It's often much easier to sacrifice something than it is to obey in a particular matter, but sacrifice is never a substitute for obedience.

During my time at Bible college, my dorm steward noticed my passion for surfing. He suggested I give up surfing because I was too passionate about it. He had good intentions, although I feel that his suggestion was misguided. But the Lord used that conversation to bring to life 1 Samuel 15:22. At first I was quite frustrated with my dorm steward. I felt in my heart he was wrong, but I wrestled in my head over the thought of what if he was right. I even got to a place where I was about to quit surfing in order to "work" for the Lord more.

Thankfully, the Lord showed me my error. He began to show me the truth of 1 Samuel 15:22, that the Lord didn't want me to sacrifice surfing for Him; He wanted me to obey Him with surfing. I realized surfing was a gift, a tool, like Moses' staff. It was not sacrifice He was seeking but rather obedience. In many ways it would have been easier to sacrifice surfing than to obey the Lord and relinquish my identity in surfing. He made me passionate about surfing because He intended to use surfing in my life as an instrument, but I must always keep my identity in Christ, not in surfing. Whatever our passions and gifts are, we must never give them more importance than what they were intended for.

Obedience has a far-reaching impact in our spiritual lives. When we disobey in a particular matter, our spiritual view in a totally unrelated matter is often blurred as a result. And the opposite is just as true; when we obey in a particular matter, we often find clarity in areas of our lives that seem unrelated to the matter we obeyed in. But obedience is connected to every aspect of a Christian's life. One of the most obvious examples of this is the account of Adam and Eve in the garden of Eden. By disobeying the Lord in the matter of eating the fruit, Adam and Eve unwittingly brought upon the entire human race the sin nature and created a divide between man and God. Do not be fooled into thinking that obedience is simply something children must learn to be mature adults. It is a constant and ever-present choice we must make as long as we live. It is a moment-by-moment decision, a surrendering of our will to the Father's.

Oswald Chambers puts it this way: "Obey God in the thing He shows you, and instantly the next thing is opened up. One reads tomes on the work of the Holy Spirit, when five minutes of drastic obedience would make things as clear as a sunbeam."[3] The reality is that obedience to Christ will impact every aspect of our lives and will have a tremendous impact in the lives of others.

---

[3] Oswald Chambers, *My Utmost For His Highest* (Ohio: Barbour Publishing, Inc., 1963), October 10.

THE IMPACT OF OBEDIENCE

We can see the powerful impact of obedience in Acts 8.

> Philip went down to the city of Samaria and began proclaiming Christ to them. The crowds with one accord were giving attention to what was said by Philip, as they heard and saw the signs which he was performing … So there was much rejoicing in that city … But an angel of the Lord spoke to Philip saying, "Get up and go south to the road that descends from Jerusalem to Gaza." (This was a desert road). (Acts 8:5–6, 8, 26)

Philip was in the midst of a very fruitful time of ministry in Samaria when the Lord told him to leave and "go south to the road that descends from Jerusalem to Gaza." In effect, the Lord told Philip to leave a thriving ministry in Samaria to go to the desert. I'm sure Philip must have been wondering if the Lord knew what He was doing as he obediently set out toward the desert road. But Philip's obedience resulted in the salvation of a very influential man in the nation of Ethiopia. Like ripples in a pond, the effect of Philip's obedience spread far and wide, and the gospel of Jesus reached a people who had not heard it yet. The same is true when we obey the Lord. Though we might not understand from our perspective, we can rest assured that He has a plan, and our obedience ushers in His purposes in our lives and the lives of others.

APPLICATION QUESTIONS

1) Where do we find our identity?
2) What is more important, obedience or sacrifice?

PHOTO BY COLIN NEARMAN

CHAPTER 7

THE HEART OF THE MATTER

While He was saying these things to them, a synagogue official came and bowed down before Him, and said, "My daughter has just died; but come and lay Your hand on her and she will live." (Matthew 9:18)

DIRE STRAIGHTS

By bowing at Jesus' feet and publicly declaring his faith in Jesus, the synagogue official was risking his reputation, his social status, his religious status, and even his own livelihood. He could possibly have been excommunicated from the synagogue for such a declaration. But his love for his daughter and his desire for her to live far outweighed anything that might keep him from doing whatever it would take to save her.

Faced with this desperate circumstance, the man knew exactly what needed to be done; he needed Jesus. And when he finally surrendered his pride, his worrying about what others would think of him, and his desire for societal status, he had a personal encounter with the living God, and he was no longer hindering his daughter from being saved. He fell at Jesus' feet, realizing that salvation only comes from Him. Sometimes the Lord will allow us to go through the valley of the shadow of death so we might grow closer to Him, and in the process He gives us a personal encounter with our precious Savior. However dire our situation may seem, we can confidently trust that Christ will guide us through it.

IT'S PERSONAL

Many don't realize that discipleship comes with a warning. Jesus said concerning discipleship, "For which one of you, when he wants to build a tower, does not first sit down and calculate the cost to see if he has enough to complete it?" (Luke 14:28). Jesus was emphatic about this. Discipleship is not merely adherence to a doctrine or devotion to a lifestyle; it is relational and personal.

Jesus was God in human form so He had all the resources imaginable. If He wanted, He could have simply hired people to spread His message of love and forgiveness, but what good would that do? Change doesn't happen unless it takes root in a person's inner man, where it becomes personal and has the opportunity to grow and blossom. This is why Jesus invested in His disciples. I don't believe God simply wants converts; He wants sons and daughters. It's astounding to me that the God of the universe calls us His children and desires to have that sort of intimate, family relationship with us. "See how great a love the Father has bestowed on us, that we should be called children of God; and such we are" (1 John 3:1). When it is personal, then discipleship is real.

Imagine what Jesus' first disciples must have been going through as Jesus was being crucified. For three years or more, they had spent their lives devoted to Jesus. They forsook their livelihoods at home to follow Jesus wherever He went. They experienced the divine power of God Almighty in the person of Jesus firsthand. Jesus had raised people from the dead in their very midst; He had performed miracles no man had ever done before. He stood in stark contrast to the religious leaders of His day, who walked in great pride and arrogance. Jesus walked in humility and love, teaching that all men are loved and desired by God.

The disciples believed Jesus when He told them He was the Messiah. They knew He was the Promised One. But they still had yet to fully understand the divine plan described throughout Scripture that prophesied of the necessity of Jesus' sacrificial death. They were following their own line of thought that Jesus was instituting a political kingdom. Scripture tells us that when Jesus tried to explain the way events would transpire concerning His death, they could not understand it; they were still earthly minded. Their faith was not intimately personal enough yet.

As the redemption of mankind was taking place, the disciples were experiencing a state of despair they had never known before. Despite all the miracles Jesus had done in the disciples' midst, and despite Jesus plainly telling them He was going to die and would rise from the dead three days later, still they doubted.

I would imagine they likely felt as though Jesus had fooled them, as if everything they believed in had been a hoax. But during this time when it seemed as though their Savior had abandoned them, He was in fact accomplishing the very thing they hoped for. At the very time when Jesus seemed furthest from them, He was actually making a way for them to be eternally united. I find this comforting. Oftentimes when we seem to have lost all hope and life seems like a cruel joke, God is at work doing something far greater than we can imagine. And the end result is a faith and relationship with Jesus that is world changing.

After Jesus' resurrection, He again spent time with His disciples. He ate with them, He talked with them, He imparted understanding to them, and He even let them touch His scars from the crucifixion. He once again showed them how much He loved them and how much He desired to have a personal relationship with them. They were not merely proselytes; they were His family, and He cared for them. The incomprehensible love that God has for us and His unwavering desire for intimacy with us was proven on the cross. The disciples no longer needed to understand every detail in life. They now understood the one thing that mattered most—God's eternal love and desire for us.

The time they spent with Jesus after His resurrection was so real and impacted them so much that they would literally die for their relationship with Him.

Their faith in Jesus and their relationship with Him was no longer simply head knowledge or devotion to a teacher or doctrine; it was extremely personal. They now had the revelation that Jesus not only provided redemption from sin, but that by being in His presence, the very purpose for living is found.

WHEN OCEANS RISE

Jesus promised He would always be with those who believe in Him, and as His assurance of this promise, He gives His Holy Spirit to anyone who receives Him. Just like Jesus' first disciples, we can be assured that no matter what sort of trials we face in life, God is there with us in the midst of them, guiding us and comforting us through them. As we experience life with Jesus in a personal way, we will find, just like the disciples did, that in His presence are all the answers we need.

But the reality is that everything I've shared so far doesn't make a difference if we don't have a personal relationship with Jesus. That relationship is the only relationship that undoubtedly has an eternal impact on our lives. All of our other relationships might affect the course of our lives, but a relationship with Jesus affects the course of our destiny and eternity. One of the most remarkable truths I've experienced in my relationship with Jesus is that He is concerned with every aspect of my life here and now. He has a specific plan and purpose for each of our lives, and as we grow closer to Him, we begin to see Him unfold it for us firsthand. It's not about joining a church or religion; it is about getting to know the only one who can truly satisfy the thirst of our souls.

I remember a coworker asked me one time what my plans for the weekend were. I answered that I was planning on attending church on Sunday. My coworker's response was, "Oh, so you're religious?"

I sort of enjoy when I get asked that question because I get a chance to explain a little bit about what I feel was one of Jesus' main messages—that God desires relationship, not religion. My response to my coworker was, "No, not really. I just have a relationship with Jesus."

Religion can't speak to a person's heart, remove a person's guilt, cleanse a person's conscience, or bless a person's life. But a relationship with Jesus does. When I found myself trapped in that cave, it wasn't religion or piety that saved me; it was God. When I sat in that prayer chapel hopeless and lonely, it wasn't a code of ethics or a list of good deeds that comforted my soul and lifted me out of the depression of loneliness; it was God. And when I finally found peace and fulfillment in this life, it wasn't from following a set of regulations or from achieving a desired social status; it was from finally starting a real and heartfelt relationship with Jesus Christ. Jesus is offering something that no religion or person in this world can offer. He is offering hope, and His hope will not disappoint.

Life with Jesus is an amazing journey, though not always an easy one. Everyone will have hardships in life, but those who face them with Jesus are guaranteed the victory. When oceans rise, we can be sure He won't let us drown.

APPLICATION QUESTIONS

1) When is discipleship real in a person's life?
2) Who did Jesus promise to give to everyone who believes in Him? What does this mean for the one who follows Jesus?

PHOTO BY CHRIS BURKARD

Contributing Photographers

www.chrisburkard.com

www.colinnearman.com

www.mattluskphotography.com

AUTHOR BIOGRAPHY

Daniel Hamlin is a writer and surfer from the central coast of California. He's worked with Walking On Water ministries, Christian Surfers International, as well as a number of missions organizations. He's appeared in many surfing publications, including *Surfer*, *The Surfer's Journal*, and *The Surfer's Path*. You can follow his blog at www.oceansandink.com

Printed in the United States
By Bookmasters